To Merry, Mabel and Joe with love   L.H.

First published in the United Kingdom in 2000 by The Chicken House, Frome, Somerset, UK

Designed by Lisa and Ellie Sturley.
Twinkle, Twinkle Little Star was written by Jane Taylor 1783-1824.

Library of Congress Cataloging-in-Publication Data available

ISBN 0-439-29656-0

10 9 8 7 6 5 4 3 2 1   01 02 03 04 05

Printed and bound in Singapore

First American edition, September 2001

Twinkle, Twinkle
Little Star

pictures by
Lesley Harker

The Chicken House

SCHOLASTIC INC.
New York

Twinkle, Twinkle, little star,

How I wonder what you are!

Up above the
world so high,
Like a diamond
in the sky.

When the blazing sun is gone,
When he nothing shines upon,
Then you show your little light,

Twinkle, Twinkle all the night.

Then the traveler in the dark,
Thanks you for your tiny spark,
He could not see which way to go,
If you did not twinkle so.

In the dark blue sky you keep,
And often through my curtains peep,
For you never shut your eye,
Till the sun is in the sky.

As your bright and tiny spark,
Lights the traveler in the dark –
Though I know not what you are,
Twinkle, Twinkle, little star.